A+ books

TORNADOES
BE AWARE AND PREPARE

by Martha E. H. Rustad

Consultant:
Joseph M. Moran, PhD
Meteorology, Professor Emeritus
University of Wisconsin-Green Bay

CAPSTONE PRESS
a capstone imprint

A+ Books are published by Capstone Press,
1710 Roe Crest Drive, North Mankato, Minnesota 56003
www.capstonepub.com

Library of Congress Cataloging-in-Publication Data
Rustad, Martha E. H. (Martha Elizabeth Hillman), 1975–
 Tornadoes : be aware and prepare / by Martha E. H. Rustad ; editor Jill Kalz.
   pages cm — (A+ books. Weather aware)
 Summary: "Describes how tornadoes form, their effects, and how people can prepare for them"—Provided
by publisher.
 Includes index.
 Audience: K-3.
 ISBN 978-1-4765-9906-9 (library binding)
 ISBN 978-1-4765-9911-3 (eBook PDF)
1. Tornadoes—Juvenile literature. I. Kalz, Jill. II. Title.
 QC955.2.R84 2015
 551.55'3—dc23   2014006649

Editorial Credits
Jill Kalz, editor; Lori Bye, designer; Svetlana Zhurkin, media researcher; Tori Abraham, production specialist

Photo Credits
Dreamstime: Alexey Stiop, 3 (middle right), 29; Getty Images: A. T. Willett, cover, 16, Cultura Science/Jason
Persoff Stormdoctor, 6–7, Jim Reed, 10–11, Joe Raedle, 27; iStockphotos: sshepard, 25; Newscom: MCT/Brandon
Wade, cover (inset); Shutterstock: Arun Roisri, 2 (middle left), 15, borsvelka (background), 2 and throughout,
Dean Kerr, 22, Hallgerd, 5, Jessica Kuras, 2 (left), 4, 26, John Huntington, 13, John Wollwerth, 2 (middle right),
8–9, 10, Lisa F. Young, 24, Matt Jeppson, 3 (middle left), 18–19, Melanie Metz, 17, Minerva Studio, 3 (left), 14,
R. Gino Santa Maria, 3 (right), 21, 28, Todd Shoemake, 1, 2 (right), 12, Zffoto (background), back cover and
throughout

Note to Parents, Teachers, and Librarians
This Weather Aware book uses full-color photographs and a nonfiction format to introduce the concept
of tornadoes. *Tornadoes: Be Aware and Prepare* is designed to be read aloud to a pre-reader or to be read
independently by an early reader. Photographs help listeners and early readers understand the text and
concepts discussed. The book encourages further learning by including the following sections: Table of
Contents, Critical Thinking Using the Common Core, Glossary, Read More, Internet Sites, and Index.
Early readers may need assistance using these features.

Printed in the United States of America in North Mankato, Minnesota
032014   008087CGF14

TABLE OF CONTENTS

BE WEATHER AWARE

Most of the time, we know what the weather will do. It follows a pattern. But sometimes the pattern changes. To keep yourself safe, be weather aware. Here you'll learn about tornadoes so you can better prepare for them.

WHAT IS A TORNADO?

A tornado is a tube of fast, spinning air that stretches from the clouds to the ground. It's sometimes called a twister or a cyclone. Tornado winds blow at least 65 miles (105 kilometers) per hour.

Some tornadoes are narrow and look like rope. Others are wide and stretch for miles.

WHAT CAUSES TORNADOES?

Most tornadoes form inside very strong thunderstorms called supercells. Winds near the top of the supercell blow one direction. Winds near the bottom blow another direction. They blow at different speeds too.

The winds cause the clouds to rotate. The rotating clouds form a funnel shape.

The winds spin faster and faster. The tube of air must touch the ground to be called a tornado. If it doesn't, it's called a funnel cloud.

Winds inside tornadoes are the fastest on Earth. The strongest tornadoes can blow more than 200 miles (322 km) per hour.

WHERE AND WHEN DO TORNADOES FORM?

Tornadoes form everywhere on Earth, except Antarctica. Places with thunderstorms have more tornadoes. About 1,300 tornadoes happen in the United States each year. Very few cause great damage.

Tornado Alley is the place most likely to have tornadoes. It includes parts of South Dakota, Colorado, Nebraska, Kansas, Oklahoma, and Texas.

Tornadoes appear most often in the spring and fall. Many thunderstorms form then. Most tornadoes strike in the late afternoon or early evening.

WHY ARE TORNADOES DANGEROUS?

Most tornadoes touch down for only a few miles. But they can cause damage. Winds may rip off branches or tip mobile homes. Trees may be pulled out of the ground.

Very strong tornadoes are rare. They can pick up cars and debris. The flying pieces crash into other things. The debris can injure people and animals. Heavy rain, hail, and lightning may also cause lots of property damage.

People need to be careful after a tornado has passed. Damaged walls may fall. Broken glass, nails, or other debris may cover the ground. Downed power lines may spark fires.

Enhanced Fujita Tornado Damage Scale

Meteorologists rate tornadoes by the damage they do.

Rating	Wind Speed (estimated)	Damage Example
EF0	65–85 miles (105–137 km) per hour	broken branches
EF1	86–110 miles (138–177 km) per hour	mobile homes overturned
EF2	111–135 miles (178–217 km) per hour	large trees uprooted
EF3	136–165 miles (218–266 km) per hour	vehicles thrown
EF4	166–200 miles (267–322 km) per hour	houses destroyed
EF5	More than 200 miles (322 km) per hour	most buildings leveled

a Doppler radar tower

HOW DO YOU PREPARE FOR A TORNADO?

Meteorologists use radar to study where and when tornadoes might appear. They try to give people time to prepare.

Meteorologists send out watches and warnings. A tornado watch means the weather is ideal for tornadoes to form. A tornado warning means a tornado is happening now.

Prepare for tornado season by making an emergency kit. Pack the kit with food and water that will last at least three days. Include first-aid supplies, a flashlight, batteries, a weather radio, and a blanket. Practice where to go for shelter if a tornado happens.

an underground storm shelter

During tornado season, listen for watches and warnings. If you hear a watch, be aware of the weather. If you hear a warning, find shelter right away. Go to a basement, storm cellar, or safe room. Stay away from windows and outside walls.

Fewer than 10 out of 100 severe thunderstorms produce a tornado. While some tornadoes do cause lots of damage, most are not deadly. Tornadoes and other storms are a natural part of our world's weather. They can be frightening. But they don't have to be, if you're weather aware.

CRITICAL THINKING USING THE COMMON CORE

1. Describe how a tornado forms. (Key Ideas and Details)

2. Describe the damage tornadoes can cause. Next, explain how that damage may be dangerous to people and animals. (Key Ideas and Details)

3. Explain the steps you would take at your home to prepare for a tornado. (Integration of Knowledge and Ideas)

GLOSSARY

debris (duh-BREE)—the scattered pieces of something that has been broken or destroyed

funnel (FUHN-uhl)—a cone shape with an open top and bottom

meteorologist (mee-tee-ur-AWL-uh-jist)—a person who studies and predicts the weather

property (PROP-ur-tee)—a house, building, or land belonging to someone

radar (RAY-dar)—a weather tool that sends out microwaves to track the size, strength, and movement of storms

rare (RAIR)—not often seen, found, or happening

rotate (ROH-tate)—to spin around

READ MORE

Aboff, Marcie. *Tornadoes!* First Graphics: Wild Earth. North Mankato, Minn.: Capstone Press, 2012.

Adamson, Heather. *Surviving a Tornado.* Amicus Readers: Be Prepared. Mankato, Minn.: Amicus Readers, 2012.

Hamilton, S.L. *Tornadoes.* Forces of Nature. Minneapolis: ABDO Pub. Co., 2012.

INTERNET SITES

FactHound offers a safe, fun way to find Internet sites related to this book. All of the sites on FactHound have been researched by our staff.

Here's all you do:

Visit *www.facthound.com*

Type in this code: 9781476599069

Check out projects, games and lots more at
www.capstonekids.com

INDEX

ML

12-14